SHIPWRECKS

True Stories at Disaster at Sea

ROGER WESTON

Copyright © 2019 by Weston Publishing Enterprises

All rights reserved.

Contents

CHAPTER 1 *Morro Castle*..........................1
CHAPTER 2 *SS Sirio*..........................12
CHAPTER 3 *Athenia*..........................18
CHAPTER 4 *Empress of Ireland*..........................25
CHAPTER 5 *Sultana*..........................28
CHAPTER 6 *KANU MARU*..........................34
CHAPTER 7 *Wilhelm Gustloff*..........................38
CHAPTER 8 *Suevic*..........................44
CHAPTER 9 *Brother Jonathan*..........................47
CHAPTER 10 *Lexington*..........................53
CHAPTER 11 *Lusitania*..........................58
CHAPTER 12 *SS Norge*..........................63
Books by Roger Weston 69

CHAPTER 1

Panic, Mystery, and Heroism on the *Morro Castle*

Chief Radio Officer George Rogers did not look like your typical hero. He was a big, lumbering gentle giant, a slow-witted man who at times seemed lively, but at other times nodded off while talking to others. Nobody would have guessed that this man would face down elements of fire and storm—even at the risk of personal destruction in the flames—to save lives—lives of those he did not even know. Yet according to his testimony, that's what happened.

    Sometimes the most unlikely men rise to the occasion and thereby climb out of obscurity into the limelight of fame and public adulation. There was something unusual about George Rogers. Nothing in his appearance would have tagged him as a likely hero. He looked neither sharp, nor capable, or even decisive.

But when he told of the actions he took in the heat of tragedy, nobody would ever see him in same way again.

The adversity began around 3 a.m. on September 8, 1934, on a ship called the *Morro Castle*, a ship that was about to go down in history and shock the entire country, from New Jersey to Oregon.

Not everyone had the capacity to rise on a storm tide the way George Rogers said he did. In fact, on this day in 1934, every crewman was tested to the limit of his character. It began early in the evening when Captain Robert Willmott made an unusual request. He had his dinner delivered to his cabin. Soon afterward, he complained of stomach pain. Not long afterwards, the severity of his condition became apparent when a crewman found him dead in his cabin.

The timing of Captain Willmott's death could not have been worse because the crew was left in a very tough situation. Naturally, Willmott's death cast a dark pall over the ship. The crew was shaken. It was bad enough to lose a good man and friend, but with two storms bearing down on the ship—one being an unusually powerful nor'easter, the other being the western fringes of a hurricane—the loss of their captain was especially stressful. The crew had to function at a high level while manning the ship in the midst of a ferocious sea. Waves ran high and wild. Wind blew as if generated by a Herculean fan. Sheets of rain flung themselves at the ship over and over. Visibility was limited. In these conditions, a new captain was needed, and Chief Officer William *Warms assumed command.* Other officers were promoted to new positions. This would be a challenge at any time, but in storm conditions, it was especially tough to have all the officers thrust into jobs that they are unfamiliar with.

If the crew was unprepared for the struggle in which they now found themselves, most of the passengers were no better off. Obviously, they had not come on this cruise to battle the elements and overcome their own propensities for weakness and human frailty. They had come on this voyage specifically to get away from their troubles. These were the depression years, and the *Morro Castle* was one of the most luxurious passenger liners on the ocean. It ran cruises to Cuba twice-a-week. The sole purpose of these cruises was to beat the Prohibition laws. This was a party boat that offered a smorgasbord of pleasures on the way to Cuba, which was itself a garden of temptations. Passengers came to relax and party, not fight for their lives. The band played *rumbas* late into the night. Laughter and lively conversations filled the lounges. After the captain's death was announced, however, all festivities were canceled for the evening. This was the final night of the cruise, and since the public festivities were not to be, the parties moved to private quarters. Alcohol flowed freely, and this, combined with the increasingly violent rolling of the ship, brought many partiers to their knees from seasickness. Soon the parties cleared out, and many nauseated people hit the sack early.

If the passengers were ill-prepared for disaster, the ship itself was no better off. Passengers would naturally assume that even in such adverse conditions, at least the company would have taken all precautions for their safety. The company officials probably did take the precautions that they could foresee, but this was 1934, and they did not have the benefit of hindsight. They did not know that the *Morro Castle* would provide an example of failure that would lead to higher safety standards for American ships of the future. While their ship was promoted as "fireproof," it was actually more like a tinderbox. Sure, the ship had fire doors, but incomprehensibly, there was a six-inch gap above the doors. This defeated the whole point. It was like cracking open the door of a woodstove; it fanned the flames to greater intensity, like a dragon blowing fire throughout the ship. It helped turn the fire into a burning storm. At the same time, the ship had a state-of-the-art ventilation system that piped in fresh ocean air, a kind of natural air-conditioning. It seemed like a good idea, but with the unusual combination of conditions on this tragic night, the ventilation system turned the ship into a crematorium. It was bad enough to have heavy winds blowing on the coals outside; it was even worse to have a ventilation system doing the same thing inside.

If the ventilation worked against the odds of survival, the 42 fire hydrants were little help. They might have helped if they had worked, but the pressure was inadequate. Only a limited number of these were employed, but that was only part of the problem. Fire hydrants are of little use unless the crew is competent in their use. The crew of the *Morro Castle* was under-trained and under-drilled. This was unfortunate because the ship was built with highly flammable materials. The paint burned. The walls burned. The floors burned. It was almost as if the ship was soaked in gasoline. Ignite a ship like that in wicked winds, and what you get is a flame-blasted inferno—a funeral pyre.

Ships would be much safer after 1934, thanks to the lessons learned from the tragedy of the *Morro Castle*. Building standards were changed so that a scenario like this would not happen again. Crews were thereafter required to drill in the use of safety equipment. Non-flammable materials were required. But none of this helped the poor souls on the *Morro Castle*.

The tragic combination of a flustered crew, sea-sick passengers, high-winds, and a highly flammable ship, led to a shocking disaster at sea, but why? Ships don't just start burning for no reason. Even under these circumstances, there should have been no problem. What could possibly start a fire on the ship as it cruised eight miles off the New Jersey coast? It was reported that around 3 a.m., a crewman saw something very unusual and suspicious. Smoke was pouring out of a locker in the reading room. Upon hearing about this, Chief Officer W.F. Warms, who had taken over as captain for the deceased Robert Wilmott, sent an officer to extinguish the flames, but when the officer tried, there was an explosion that he attributed to gasoline in the locker. This is what set off the fatal fire.

Later on, Captain Warms attributed the fire in the reading room to an incendiary in the locker. He believed this because this was not the first fire on the *Morro Castle*. There had been a fire in the ship's hold during a previous voyage, and on *that* occasion, charred paper was found in the hold. The previous fire had been put out, and Warms believed this one could also be extinguished. For this reason, he delayed giving the order to send an SOS message. After a thirty minute delay, it became clear that the fire was out of control, and the SOS message was sent by George Rogers.

All told, a nightmare was just beginning on the storm-tossed cruise ship. Regardless of whether or not the officers were confused in new jobs or making bad decisions, one man acted like an unflinching hero throughout the entire ordeal. That man was Chief Radio Officer George Rogers.

Rogers was not allowed to send out an SOS without the permission of the captain; therefore, he waited patiently at his radio for over half an hour. As he told it, even as the fire raged around him, he did not break protocol. Rogers was a big heavy man, and he did not like the heat. Nevertheless, he said that he never even flinched. Nor did he flee his post and try to save himself. To the contrary, he stayed at his post, and even the probability of his own agonizing death did not deter him from his duty. The heat grew so intense, he said, that the battery which powered his receiver exploded and spilled sulfuric acid onto the floor. Fortunately, the transmitter still worked. Rogers remained poised even in this nightmarish situation. When a generator wire came loose, he calmly groped through the thick smoke and with blistering fingers, he reattached the wire. He then continued transmitting the SOS. Many lives were saved, evidently due to the steely nerves and heroic actions of Chief Radio Officer George Rogers.

Once the SOS call was made, the people had a chance, but unfortunately, the odds were still against them. There were no ships nearby, and gale-force winds were fueling the blaze. Hundreds of passengers could not even leave their cabins because the hallways were blow torches. Meanwhile, their rooms filled with black, acrid smoke. Few passengers on the lower decks had any chance of survival. For those on the upper decks, their odds were still not good. Some passengers had no chance of getting to lifeboats because the only lifeboats they could get close to were burning. At the same time, the paint on the steel decks was in flames. Wood floors were burning. Wood-paneled walls were burning. Many of the passengers did the only thing they could do. They jumped overboard, despite the fact that they were in the fringes of an Atlantic hurricane and eight miles from land. Several husbands held hands with their wives and stepped over the void. They plummeted down into the Atlantic waters on a terrifying September night. The waters weren't as cold as in the dead of winter, but this was a scary place to be. Despite the poor visibility and driving rain, their options were clear. They must swim to shore or die. There were no other options. They swam.

If they could.

The crew took every action they could to save as many passengers as possible, but panic broke out in certain places. Captain Warms told his crew to wake the passengers and even bang pots and pans if necessary. In certain areas, evacuation was an orderly affair. Elsewhere, it was just the opposite. People became irrational and acted on fear and emotion. Some were bleeding from wounds caused by exploding windows. Screams were heard. Parents lost track of their children. When Warms saw a group of passengers, he tried to save them. He told them to get into the lifeboat, but they would not obey him.

"For God's sake, get into the boats!" he shouted. He then watched in disbelief as a steward had to put a girl in one of the boats by force.

Below decks, the few passengers who were able to make a dash for the stairwells had to fight for their lives—not just against the smoke and the burning floors—but also against other passengers. One man tried three times to scramble up the narrow stairwell, but three times other men grabbed his ankles and pulled his feet out from under him. They dragged him back down so that they could beat him up the stairs and to the lifeboats.

The few who made it to the lifeboats were little better off for their struggle. As they sat in the boats, the flames moved closer and closer, but unpracticed crewmen struggled to launch the boats. After long delays, some boats were finally lowered into the wind-raked seas, but they were mostly empty except for a number of the crewmen. Most passengers had been cut off from the lifeboats by corridors of flame. They either jumped for their lives or perished in the heat. Some who jumped off the stern were sucked into the propellers and killed instantly. Others were killed as they hit the water because they had not been drilled in proper use of their life preservers. They needed to hold onto the preserver and then put it on after they were in the water. Unfortunately, many put their life vests on first and then jumped, which caused their necks to be broken on impact with the water. Those who survived the jump tread water or swam in the hurricane-thrashed Atlantic.

Out in the ocean, the survivors would have to stay afloat for hours if they had any prayer of making it. Surrounded by a flotsam of debris and dead bodies, they kept their morale up by singing or making jokes. It wasn't all fun and games, however. Some survivors reported sharks circling in the waters. One woman was filled with terror for another reason. She feared that sea gulls would pluck out her eyes. As she floated for hours, she clung to her last $40 and prayed out loud that the seagulls would spare her.

It was tough, but some persevered through it all. George Watremez drifted in the savage seas for eight hours before he was finally rescued by the *Paramount*, a fishing boat owned by the Bogan family who'd battled the storm to get out there and help victims of the disaster.

A Cuban boy swam for shore. Never mind that he was rising and falling with the waves; he just swam as if it was the most normal thing to do.

Mrs. Edward Brady stayed close to her husband for seven hours. Finally, her man could not go on. His strength ran out. He pushed her away and told her to save herself. She then suffered the horror of watching her husband go under. A few minutes later she was rescued.

The Coast Guard and police fought their own epic battles against the sea in their efforts to navigate their boats far enough out to rescue survivors from the smoking leviathan. Tragically, the ferocious gale and savage waters proved too much. Many boats had to turn back in failure.

Although it took a few hours for the nearest ships to arrive and lend help, a few did make it in time to save lives. The first ship on the scene was the cruise liner *Monarch of Bermuda*. She rescued over 65 people. Fortunately, the *Andrea F. Luckenbach* was not far behind, and she brought on another 22 desperate souls.

The *President Cleveland* and the *City of Savannah* also showed up, but despite their efforts, they were not able to spot any bodies or survivors.

Eight lifeboats from the stricken ship made their way to shore despite a deluge of rain and being constantly swamped by waves and battered by winds. Sadly, the lifeboats only carried 85 people, mostly crew.

After a six hour swim, Mr. and Mrs. Abraham Cohen crawled up on the beach. They were one of two couples that survived the swim to shore.

The bodies of the others were spotted in the waters off of Sandy Hook, N.J.

The *Morro Castle* is one of the more tragic shipwrecks on record. The list of casualties included 137 names.

But thanks to the radio operator George Rogers, the man who fought death unflinchingly while awaiting orders, other ships did arrive and search for survivors. George was the man who sent the critical SOS.

Rogers later told investigators that "My feet were burning and the towel around my face had become impregnated with smoke. The corner of the table exploded and the room filled with sulphuric fumes."

Rogers, the main hero of the disaster, soon became the hero of the subsequent investigations, of which he became the star witness. He was a fountain of testimony against the officers of the *Morro Castle*. His selfless story painted a dishonorable picture of these officers.

George Rogers became an American icon for his unmatched heroism. He later parlayed his hero status into a gig on Broadway, where for two weeks he amazed audiences with his spectacular tale of unflinching courage. After the Broadway show ran its course, Rogers faded into obscurity—at least for a while. He opened a radio repair shop, but struggled to make ends meet. Then, mysteriously, a fire destroyed his business. The Bayonne Police Department conducted an arson investigation, but could not prove anything.

Evidently, George Rogers was haunted by tragedy. It was learned that he had a long criminal record that included convictions for theft. There had been other issues as well. Six years previously, a fire had broken out at the Wireless Egert Company, where he was employed at the time. Although he was a suspect, nothing was ever proven.

It also came to light that prior to his untimely death, Captain Wilmott had been acting strangely. He had feared a plot against his life due to a dangerous radical onboard his ship. The radical was none other than George Rogers' assistant in the radio room. His name was George Alanga. Rogers didn't defend his right-hand man at all when Captain Wilmott told him about his fears. On the contrary, Rogers said that he had found two vials of a mysterious liquid in Alanga's locker. However, Rogers also said that he had thrown the vials overboard, so he no longer had the evidence. Captain Wilmott had been terrified of Alanga because the extremist was involved in a labor dispute against the company. He had even tried to lead a strike against the shipping line. Furthermore, Wilmott had just fired Alanga, who was scheduled to leave the ship permanently in New York. The captain also had suspicions against Rogers, but at that time, he'd needed Rogers as a witness against Alanga.

Nothing was ever proved against Alanga. There was bad blood between him and the captain and the company, but little else is known. It's possible that he was framed, but for now, the mystery lives on. After the shipwreck and the investigation, some questioned whether everything was just as the heroic George Rogers had said or whether he might have left a few things out of his amazing story.

Despite Rogers' checkered past, he managed to secure a position at the Bayonne Police Department when they needed a radio man to assist Vincent Doyle. Unfortunately, Doyle had gotten bad vibes from Rogers and asked a lot of questions about the *Morro Castle*. Things were said on both sides that made George Rogers uncomfortable. Shortly thereafter, Doyle received a package in the mail. Friends often asked him to repair things, so his guard was down. This time a heater for a fish tank needed fixing. When Doyle plugged it in, a bright flash accompanied an explosion. Doyle was severely injured, but he survived. The package was traced back to George Rogers. Rogers was sentenced to at least twelve years in the big house for attempted murder; however, he managed to fly the coop on parole after only four years based on a program that would allow him to serve in the military as an alternative to finishing his sentence.

However, the Navy rejected George. Too bad, but at least he was a free man now. He borrowed $7,500 from a friend named William Hummel. When Hummel decided to move to Florida and needed his money back, he pressured Rogers to pay up. A month later, Hummel's body was found next to his daughter's. They'd been bludgeoned to death with a blunt object.

This time George Rogers was sentenced to life in prison. He died behind bars four years later from a heart attack.

This was an abysmal end for the 'hero' of the *Morro Castle* shipwreck. In hind-sight, there were some who came to question whether or not Rogers was really a hero of the *Morro Castle,* after all? Was it possible that the steel-nerved radio man might have actually had something to do with the fire on the popular cruise ship? Theories suggested that perhaps Rogers poisoned the captain and started the fire to cover up the murder. What motive could there have been for such an improbable scenario?

In 1988, Robert J. McDonnell did extensive research of the public records and uncovered information that the government had kept under lock and key. While much information was still withheld for undisclosed reasons, McDonnell concluded that Captain Wilmot was definitely not murdered. Instead, the steamship company was in financial trouble. They'd probably hired Rogers to light the fire so that they could collect millions in insurance money.

McDonnell also discovered a reason why the government might have kept the records sealed even when innocent men, including the stand-in Captain Wilmott, were convicted of willful negligence by a federal appeals court. McDonnell says federal investigators suspected arson all along, but they failed to act because the incredible George Rogers was a federal informant. It's not entirely clear what he was informing on. However, the Ward line had profitable federal mail contracts and was involved in the illicit trafficking of arms to Cuban rebels.

This new theory conflicts with the theories of previous writers who, without the benefit of the certain withheld information, suggested that perhaps Rogers poisoned the captain and started the fire to cover up the murder. McDonnell shoots this theory down. However, he falls short of reinstating the hero status of radio operator George Rogers.

Whatever was really going on, the shipwreck of the *Morro Castle* appears to be a twisted tale, but worse than that, it was a tragic tale for all the families of the deceased—the many, many families.

CHAPTER 2

High Tragedy at Sea

The Italian merchant steamer, *SS Sirio*, departed from Genoa on August 2, 1904, starting on a voyage that the Italian immigrants onboard believed would be a restful and peaceful ride to begin their new lives in Argentina. After picking up additional passengers in Barcelona, Spain, the ship, with almost 800 souls on board, set out for South America on August 4. However, she did not get far at all. In fact, she was only 2 ½ miles east of Cape Palos near Cartagena, Spain when she ran aground at full-speed on a reef off Hormigas Island.

Fishermen had taken notice of the *SS Sirio*, which was cruising close by in tricky waters. They heard a tremendous crashing noise when the ship hit a reef. They saw passengers knocked off their feet from the impact, falling hard onto the *SS Sirio*'s steel decks. For the fishermen, it was a grim moment to see the brutal crash. However, in the next four minutes, that moment of shock melted into a surreal experience as they watched the ship's stern rapidly sink below the rippling, pulsating surface of the shiny blue waters. Fortunately, these fishermen were not passive men. They knew the sea as well as they knew their own mothers, maybe better. They were also highly competent on the waters. Realizing that a disaster was unfolding, they flew into action. They needed little urging; however, they got some anyway. The stern of the *SS Sirio* sank so quickly that within just four minutes, it was underwater, and the fishermen could hear the screams of the drowning. The bow was still above the surface, like a dolphin sticking its nose out of the water.

While the fishermen began their rescue efforts, a truly tragic, life-and-death drama was playing out on board ship. By one account, the captain was not on the bridge when the ship struck the reef; rather, he'd turned over the helm to an inexperienced third mate. If so, this was one of a series of misjudgments, which is surprising. After all, the captain had 46 years experience and a flawless record. This was his final voyage before retirement. Perhaps he let his guard down and decided to relax a little on this last trip. Forty-six years experience. Flawless record. Hundreds of thousands of sea captains never achieved such an impressive record. Captain Giuseppe Piccone could sail a ship from Spain to Argentina in his sleep if he had to. Not, however, on this particular day, this most tragic day.

The fishermen and the passengers on the *SS Sirio* weren't the only players in this epic tragedy. There was a full cast, and all the actors were on hand. There were other ships in the area. One of those vessels was the French steamer *Marie Louise*. Her captain saw the whole disaster unfold. He saw the *SS Sirio* on a risky course through a dangerous area when she crashed into a submerged obstacle. The bow of the doomed ship rose up out of the water like a breaching whale. The boiler exploded. It erupted like Mount Vesuvius, a tremendous explosion. Screams were heard. Bodies were suddenly floating past the *Marie Louise*.

"I want a boat in the water now," the captain of the Marie Louise ordered. "Save anyone you can."

Over on the *SS Sirio*, Captain Giuseppe Piccone had a different perspective because it was his ship that was sinking. One thing Piccone lacked, thankfully for his forty-six years of passengers, was experience in dealing with shipwrecks and calamity. For *forty-six years*, he had avoided trouble. Conflicting accounts emerged in the press as to what happened on this fateful day. Some said the captain froze; others testified that panic broke out and he tried to contain it, but couldn't. The captain himself later confessed that his actions were imprudent.

Why would a captain with 46 years experience take imprudent actions? Why would he take a course that was obviously dangerous according to the captain of the *Marie Louise*? The *SS Sirio* was not just any ship. Her entire career had been devoted to delivering immigrants from Italy and Spain to South America. She had safely helped over 170,000 immigrants begin new lives in Argentina. Thousands and thousands of people had fond memories of this ship. It is reported, however, that these were not all legal immigrants.

The *SS Sirio* was known to frequently make unofficial stops along the coast of Spain where illegal immigrants were taken aboard for a steep price. These illegal immigrants made the trans-Atlantic journeys more profitable. Easy profits are enough to sway owners and captains to take extra risks.

In life, it is said that the toughest trees are those that must survive in the wind because they must grow the stoutest roots in order to withstand the harsh elements. As stated, Captain Giuseppe

Piccone had enjoyed a smooth career. According to the press, when the tragedy sprung upon him, he froze, he choked, he couldn't function. He was among the first to abandon ship.

Seeing the captain flee naturally distressed the hundreds passengers. Chaos broke out on deck. As the stern quickly sank, passengers scrambled for the bow. They fought to get there first. They fought for real estate because prices were rising quickly.

They fought viciously. Fear rode on their backs. Pandemonium reigned. Primitive instincts ruled. Passengers who hours earlier treated each other as new friends now trampled over each other to save themselves. While attempts were made to deploy lifeboats, fights broke out—knife fights. This was truly survival of the fittest. It didn't occur over millions of years; it played out in a matter of a few desperate minutes. *Even fights to the death.* Passengers were spared drowning because they were murdered in bloody brawls. The knowledge of economics proved less valuable than the knowledge brute violence. Awful sounds carried across the waters—shouts of men, screams of women, and cries of children. The pretenses of civilized man were stripped away, revealing raw, savage survival instincts.

While some behaved badly under pressure, others responded differently. The Bishop of Sao Pablo was blessing the drowning passengers as the ship went down. That is how he died. A monk died while kneeling on deck in prayer. The Austrian Consul to Rio de Janeiro leapt overboard in a life belt, but when he came across a mother and child about to give up to the sea, he gave them his life vest. He then tried to fight the currents and swim for land without it. When a boat pulled him from the water, they said he was exhausted. Had they not saved him, he might well have perished.

A young mother clinging to her baby was told, *"Dump the child, you fool! Save yourself!"*

"Never," she cried. "We'll die together!" As it turned out, they were among the survivors.

There were many survivors because various ships and trawlers in the area steamed to their rescue. One of these was the trawler *Joven Miguel*. The crew of the *Joven Miguel*, however, panicked and wanted to break away from the rescue because they feared they would be overloaded and sink. Facing a mutiny, the captain drew his pistol and shouted, "As long as it's possible to take on another passenger, we will not move." Fearing the captain more than the sea, they returned to the rescue.

As they took on more swimmers, the captain realized that they were becoming top heavy and might very well capsize. He ordered the survivors below decks, but they were still gripped with fear and refused. The captain brought out his pistol again. He waved it around in the air. "Get below now or I'll shoot you and throw you back into water." The passengers, having just been rescued, now realized that they were at the mercy of a gun-wielding madman. They hurried below, which steadied the boat and kept her safe from capsizing. The madman saved 300 lives.

Another trawler, the *Vicenta Llicano* hauled out 200 people. An old man in a dinghy saved twelve more.

The fishermen along the coast sent out boats to rescue passengers. Some of those big-hearted mariners overloaded their boats with people. As a result, their boats overturned, dooming the fishermen along with those they had tried to save.

When all the survivors were brought ashore, a whole new tragic drama began. Parents who'd been separated from their children wept bitterly upon learning that their children were missing. One woman couldn't take the agony and heartbreak. Her mental faculties fragmented. She literally went insane over her lost child. Many rescued children realized that their parents had died, leaving them as orphans. As they looked out to sea, they saw their parents' graves. As they looked around on land, they saw their own scary, lonely futures.

In some cases, spirits were broken by adversity. Some of the survivors gave up their dreams of immigrating to Argentina. They resolved to return—by land—to their homeland—for good.

All told, 300 people died in the shipwreck of the *SS Sirio*. A year later, it was reported that Captain Giuseppe Piccone died of grief.

CHAPTER 3

Athenia: First Sinking in World War Two's Battle of the Atlantic

In October of 1939, the Nazi party's official newspaper, the *Voelkischer Beobachter* broke the story that England had intentionally sunken the cruise ship *Athenia* in order to blame Germany and draw the U.S. into the war as an ally. It was a shocking revelation that England—for political reasons—had sunk a passenger ship with over 1,100 passengers on it, mostly women and children. There were also 311 unfortunate Americans.

Germany's accusation against Britain was not just a vague reference in a side bar of the *Voelkischer Beobachter;* it was specific. It singled out Winston Churchill, then First Lord of the Admiralty and accused him of masterminding the diabolical plot.

In America, US Senator Robert Rice Reynolds, among others, claimed that Britain may have wanted to "infuriate the

American people", which is why they sank a ship with hundreds of Americans on board.

The *Athenia*'s passengers, of course, had not been worried about Churchill sinking a British ship. Nobody would have thought that he would do such a thing.

The *Athenia* had departed from Glasgow on Friday, September 1, 1939—destination Montreal, Canada. England had just declared war on Germany hours before, and many Americans—at the encouragement of the British government—secured their tickets on the *Athenia* to return to America and flee the war. Ironically, they were about to become its first victims.

Most people who boarded the ship expected a safe trip. After all, they were heading *away from* Europe where trouble was brewing. They were heading *towards* safety. The ship itself was a peaceful place, a wonderful place to be. In many respects it was just another cruise; however, the travelers did notice a few disturbing signs. For one, the windows were all painted black to hide any light; in addition, smoking was prohibited on deck. Nobody was allowed to even light a match on deck. Third, the ship sailed a zigzag course to foil any submarine attack—presumably by German U-boats.

Other than these minor details, it was life as usual on the *Athenia*. Although one crewman was convinced he would never live to see America, this was not the general sentiment. It was a happy, social time, a time of meeting people in dining rooms, of relaxing and reading good books. In some respects, life didn't get any better than this. They had caught the only ship out, and they were safe! Children walked happily on deck, enjoying the novel experience. Games were played. Church services were held.

The sense of relief and excitement didn't last long, however. In less than 24 hours, a massive explosion rocked the boat; it ripped through the engine room and blasted the cargo hatch high into the air including people that were sitting on it. These people landed on deck blackened and lifeless. Mrs. James Orr, along with her one-year-old daughter, were blasted against the railing; they survived but with injuries. Crude oil sprayed out of broken pipes.

In the kitchen, two huge vats of boiling oil spilled onto two cooks, burning them severely. Out in the dining area, one woman had just dipped her spoon into her bowl of soup, but that's as far as her hand ever got.

In the accommodations area, half-dressed people filled smoky passageways that smelled of cordite. In the darkness, they felt the water level rising up their legs. Their knees bumped into floating debris. A stairwell had been eviscerated, leaving some people to climb from edge-to-edge to work their way up to the main deck.

The ship began to list, causing the lifeboats to hang at awkward angles. Nevertheless, people who had survived the blast and made it outside gathered around the lifeboats. They had been through the emergency drill, so there was some sense of order, but there were also outbreaks of panic.

Women and children were supposed to board lifeboats first, but at one lifeboat station, a number of men feared there would be no space left for them. They shoved aside the women and children and tried to claim their seats by force. A crewman manning that lifeboat fought them back by wielding an ax.

As one of the lifeboats was lowered, a rope broke. Mrs. Orr and her daughter, who'd just been blasted against the railing, now barely survived another traumatic event as the lifeboat crashed down into the water. Now, despite her cracked ribs, Ms. Orr began bailing with their shoes, a chore that would continue on through a long, dark and very cold night.

Not everyone stayed active. Many of the people in the lifeboats were miserable. They were sick from the gas that was released in the explosion and seasick from the rocky ocean. Many were only half dressed. One woman was dressed in nothing but a satin nightgown. Hypothermia set in for those who had been forced to jump in the ocean or who had been thrown out of their lifeboat during the rough launchings.

"Look!" a woman said, pointing. "A submarine."

A German U-boat opened fire on the ship's wireless antennas. It then approached the scattered lifeboats. The boats were spread out around the sinking ship, spread out for just this reason—in case a submarine showed up and tried to machine gun the survivors.

The U-boat approached long enough for the captain to get a good look at the ship. Then it turned tail and stole away into the night.

"Help us!" a woman cried out. "We'll die out here!"

The U-boat did not stick around to save a single person. Her German commander, with his submarine now safely beneath the surface, was in shock. He had thought that the ship he had attacked was an armed merchant cruiser. After dealing the fatal blow, he'd approached to identify the ship for his log entry. When he checked the ship against the Lloyd's Register, he was sickened to realize that he'd just sunk an unarmed cruise ship. This was against all prize rules of warfare, for both Britain and Germany. Commander Lemp realized he had made a horrible mistake.

As Lemp stole away in his U-boat, he was in a state of disbelief. He'd been sure of his conclusion. The ship had been acting like a warship. It had been blacked out and was following a zigzag course. Plus, it was following an unusual course for a passenger ship. He began to sweat profusely. He feared he could face a court marshal back in Germany. He feared what would happen when Admiral Donitz learned of this. Lemp decided then and there that he must hide his fatal error. He forced his crew to take an oath of secrecy and never speak of what had occurred. As for his log entry, he never made it. The event never officially happened.

Up on the surface, the people in the lifeboats were miserable and shaking in the cold because of what had happened, and they were the lucky ones. Many had been killed in the explosion. For the survivors, it was a night of suffering.

One woman, Mrs. Rhonda Thomas or Rochester, New York, had been well dressed because she'd been out on deck. A naked baby was handed to her to keep under her coat. The baby had no relatives in the boat. Mrs. Thomas and another woman shared duties, alternately rowing and sheltering the infant.

Unidentified bodies floated by in the water. It was enough to plunge a person into deep depression and despair, the sort that weakened the individual's propensity for survival. People dealt with their grief in different ways. Some women and children cried. Others endured the pain of serious injuries. A cook was not expected to live from his burns. He was in a miserable state. People did what they had to do to adjust and keep their morale up. Some prayed while others sung hymns. Women bailed with their shoes and found that keeping busy kept their mind off their fate. By morning, some of the people had died.

Then ships began to arrive on the scene. The Sweedish yacht *Southern Cross*, the US cargo ship *City of Flint*, the Norwegian tanker *Knute Nelson*, and the US destroyers *Electra* and *Escort* all showed up to rescue survivors. Rope ladders were thrown over the sides of ships. Those who could climb did so. Others were raised by rope. Many lives were saved, but there were also accidents. Some of the 'survivors' fell and were crushed to death between their lifeboat and rescue ship when the waves lifted and lunged the smaller boats against the bigger ones. Fifty people died when one of the lifeboats was crushed under the propeller of the tanker *Knute Nelson*. While there was sadness, there was also relief. Together, the rescue ships saved 981 lives while the US destroyer *Fame* did an anti-submarine sweep during the rescue operations.

In Germany, Admiral Donitz learned of the sinking from the BBC. Hitler was furious, but he decided to cover it up. Lemp's war diary was falsified. Hitler denied Germany's role and used the incident as propaganda, blaming England to hopefully drive a wedge between England and America.

Commander Lemp went on to sink twenty more ships. Finally, he was killed when his German U-boat was severely damaged by depth charges. He surfaced, and before destroying classified materials, he ordered his men to abandon the sinking ship. The sub was boarded by sailors of the *HMS Bulldog*. They did a quick search and found an infamous German encryption device—a find that soon helped America win the Atlantic war. Lemp's fate is matter of confusion. He was either shot in the water or chose to drown rather than be taken prisoner.

Either way, Lemp played a key role in World War Two history—as the man whose crucial mistake launched the Battle of the Atlantic—and as the man who caused the beginning of the end of that battle, when, thinking his ship was doomed, he failed to destroy sensitive equipment.

The Battle of the Atlantic was the longest unbroken military campaign of World War Two. It raged on from 1939 through 1945. During that time, 3,500 merchant ships and 175 warships were sunk against 783 sunken U-boats.

For the actions of one rogue, one Commander Lemp, to have had such a profound impact on the beginning and the end of the Battle of the Atlantic is truly astonishing.

CHAPTER 4

Empress of Ireland: Shipwreck in the Night

2:00 a.m. St. Lawrence River. May 29, 1914. The river was shrowded in fog. Two ships were steaming toward each other. The Canadian Pacific steamship *Empress of Ireland*, was headed outbound from Quebec. The Norwegian collier *Storstad* was heading upriver. *The Empress* was close to shore, and so was *the Storstad*. The officers on each ship spotted the other ship a distance.

Courses had to be altered. On the bridge of the Empress of Ireland, Captain Henry Kendall changed his course. Just then the two ships were swallowed in fog. Kendall blasted his whistle three times, signaling that he was ordering his engines full astern. The ship slowed and was nearly stopped. The next thing Kendall saw was masthead lights glowing out of the fog to starboard. The other ship was booming straight at him. They were so close that there was no time to move or change course. Collision was inevitable. All Kendall could do was to change his ship's angle enough to limit the damage to a glancing blow. He ordered a sharp turn to starboard. The *Storstad*'s bow smashed between the liner's steel ribs, ripping the steal and cutting an opening, in which flowed the river.

The *Empress* began to list from the rising water, and tragic consequences followed. People sleeping in starboard cabins were submerged in freezing water and died while sleeping. On deck, the situation was also dire. The new slant of her decks made the lifeboats useless. Only six of them could be deployed. After only ten minutes, the ship fell over onto her side. Hundreds of passengers climbed onto her hull and hoped for rescue. Four minutes later, the beautiful *Empress of Ireland* sank into freezing water. 1,012 perished, including 840 passengers. 465 survived after they were pulled out of the river in hypothermic condition. The death toll exceeded that of the *Titanic*.

In the dark of night, 1,012 lives came to a sudden, unexpected end in the St. Lawrence River when the *Empress of Ireland* went down.

Grace Hanagan was among the survivors. She was an eight-year-old girl, who was traveling with her parents to London to take part in the Salvation Army's International Congress. Her parents were lost. For a year afterwards, Grace hoped that her mother might have survived because her body was never found.
An entrepreneur named Edward Seybold survived, but his wife Susanna Seybold was lost. It was their 43rd wedding anniversary.
Egildo Braga and his wife Carolina survived, but it was tragic good luck. Egildo did everything he could to save his wife and son in the freezing water, but the river was too powerful. It tore away his son, who was even tied to his father. Egildo

desperately searched for his son in the darkness. He could not find him. Their son perished in the river.

Today we remember and honor the 1,012 people who entered history with the *Empress of Ireland*.

CHAPTER 5

Sultana Shipwreck: Last Tragedy of the Civil War

One of the most amazing shipwrecks in American history is largely unknown. The ship was called the *Sultana*, and she ran a route on the Mississippi River, transporting cargo and passengers. On April 27, 1865, she swung up to the docks at Vicksburg, where her lines were made fast. It was then that the engineer noticed something worrisome: the boilers were leaking. After evaluating their options, the engineers and captain decided that the boilers would be repaired straightaway.

Vicksberg, at that time, was swarming with semi-invalid civil war veterans. These Union soldiers were newly-released POWs. They'd come from various prisons where they had been sadly neglected. They were diseased, half–starved skeletons with many wounds that needed proper medical attention.

Because the Civil War had just ended eighteen days ago, the government was paying boat captains for every veteran that they shipped up river. Soldiers began boarding the *Sultana* even as it was being repaired.

Despite their sad physical condition, they were in high spirits like the Captain J.C. Mason had never seen before. They were singing, smiling, shouting, and dancing with joy. They had just gotten their lives back and were headed home. Many of them had expected to die in the camps. Now they'd literally been given a second life. They were ecstatic. There weren't just a few soldiers on the *Sultana* either. There were lots of them. They poured onto the paddle wheeler like a flood. In no time at all, the *Sultana* was full, packed well beyond capacity. In no way was she built for this many passengers. It was a dangerous situation. The *Sultana* was legally entitled to carry 376 passengers. It was presently carrying 2,300. The captain was nervous, but he did not turn away many veterans.

The engineers were lively, and they wasted no time. The boilers were quickly repaired, and the *Sultana* headed upriver, her big paddle wheels thrashing the water.

Despite being grossly overloaded and running against the current, the *Sultana* performed well for the next couple of days. At Memphis, the boiler showed more signs of leaking. Once again, repairs were done. The boat moved on, heading into the current with over five times more passengers than she was allowed to carry.

As it turned out, the current was stronger than usual. At 2 a.m., they were only a few miles upstream from Memphis. The weighed-down boat was really working hard to make progress. It was earning every inch against the flood-stage currents. Then the boilers failed. A tremendous explosion lit up the ship. It was so powerful that the boom was heard all the way back in Memphis. The detonation blew hundreds of sleeping soldiers into the river. These half-invalid men landed in freezing water, splashing down below the surface along with half of the boat's superstructure. A large portion of the boat had been obliterated. It was a miracle that men survived both the explosion and the shock of landing in the river during their sleep. Because there was wreckage in the water, many soldiers were able to grab onto some flotsam and hold on for their life. This was a rude awakening, but also a lucky one.

Sadly, many of the men could not swim and were also malnourished and weak. At the same time, pieces of wreckage were quickly claimed. When too many men tried to climb on, the wreckage was driven under water. Then panicked drowning men grabbed onto other men to use them as flotation devices. In too many cases, both men sunk and never came up. In other cases, survivors drove away those who would take them under. It was an easy choice to make to drive them off and let them drown; it was frequently a hard memory to live with.

The ice-cold water proved too much for many of the worn-out men. Hundreds of them died from the shock because they could not swim.

Back on the boat, people were fighting over lumber. They were tearing away lumber wherever they could find it. Everyone wanted a flotation device. Only the most determined were successful.

One man found a ten-foot alligator in a wooden cage. He bayoneted the beast and rolled the cage into the river. He dove in and clung to that cage until a boat picked him up. A man who been caged-up in prison now owed his life a cage.

Three other men held onto a bale of hay and floated all the way back to Memphis.

James K. Brady had awoken to find that he was on fire, or at least his clothes were. Most of his hair had burned off. He and his friend David Ettleman put out the flames on Brady, but the boat was also burning. Next, they rushed around looking for a flotation device. They had no luck, so they went to the hurricane deck, where they saw an astounding scene.

As Brady said, "Oh, what a sight met our gaze! There were some killed in the explosion, lying in the bottom of the boat, being trampled upon, while some were crying and praying. Many were cursing while others were singing. That sight I shall never forget; I often see it in my sleep, and wake with a start."

Brady and Ettleman found a gangplank, which they grabbed on just as it was going over the side. Brady later explained that "About fifteen or sixteen of us that had stuck to the plank. But now a new danger had seized me, as someone grabbed me by the right foot and it seemed as though it was in a vise; try as I would, I could not shake him off. I gripped the plank with all the strength that I had, and then I got my left foot between his hand and my foot and while holding on to the plank with both hands I pried him loose with my left foot, he taking my sock along with him... He sank out of sight and I saw him no more." Such incidents were common, but that didn't make it any easier. Anyway, Brady's troubles weren't over.

The gangplank flipped over during the struggle, and several other men were lost. Brady's spirits plummeted. He was losing hope. He was weak, having lost thirty percent of his body weight in prison. In his darkest moments, it was his friend who helped him: "Every little while he would call out some encouraging word to me to keep up my spirits."

On the burning ship, Chester Berry was fighting his own battle for survival. He got himself a piece of cabin door casing, but hesitated to jump in the water. The flames had not reached the bow yet, but the real reason was what he saw in the water. As he explained, it was "literally black with human beings, many of whom were sinking and taking others with them. Being a good swimmer, and having board enough to save me, even if I were not, I concluded to wait till the rush was over." To jump into a crowd of drowning men would have been risky.

Remaining on board a little longer gave him time to look around and see how humans responded to a situation where they were facing death, men who had faced it before, but finally thought they were getting another shot at life. Then suddenly they saw that second chance slipping away. Berry said, "The horrors of that night will never be effaced from my memory — such swearing, praying, shouting and crying I had never heard; and much of it from the same throat — imprecations followed by petitions to the Almighty, denunciations by bitter weeping."

Berry saw that different men responded differently. He saw men who would fight tooth and nail to survive. He saw one man whose flotation devices had been taken from him by stronger men, and he would not fight anymore. He could have gotten more wood from the pile, but he had had enough. He was done fighting. Berry was angry at his defeatist attitude and let him be. For years, it would haunt him that he didn't do more to help that broken man. Berry was haunted by a man who would not help himself.

Finally, the waters cleared of people, and Berry dove in. He struggled with the current for a time and on account of the ice-cold water, he became completely discouraged to the point where he decided it wasn't worth it to struggle any longer. He realized that he would drown in spite of his efforts, so it would just be easier to give up and die. He started to do just that when a miracle happened. As Berry puts it, "I was transported for the moment to 'the old house at home,' and that I was wending my way slowly up the path from the road gate to the house…as plainly as I ever heard my mother's voice. I heard it that evening." Their family had always prayed together. His mother said the prayer because his father was mute. Now Berry actually heard her pray "God save my boy."

After that, Berry's attitude changed. He knew that his mother was expecting him to return home from war and how much it meant to her. He said, "I fiercely clutched the board and hissed between my now firmly set teeth 'Mother, by the help of God, your prayer shall be answered.'"
Berry ended up clinging to a tree until a boat rescued him.

James K. Brady, whose friend's encouraging words gave him strength, was another survivor. Brady lasted till daylight and they managed to get to shore. Another man crawled ashore with them, but he was so badly burned that he died three minutes after reaching land.

1,800 other men also passed away. They had survived the Civil War, including time in POW camps. They were on their way home to see their families. But destiny had other plans.

More people died on the *Sultana* than on the *Titanic*. It is the worst shipwreck in American history, but few know of it. To some degree it was overshadowed by greater events and bigger news. Lincoln had been assassinated only a week earlier. His assassin, John Wilkes Booth had just been apprehended the previous day.

The impact on the 1800 families was no doubt profound. But these 1800 are not forgotten. We honor them for their sacrifice for their country and their fellow man. This was the last tragedy of the Civil War, but it was more than that. It was the loss of 1,800 brothers. Their story reminds us of who they were and what they did.

CHAPTER 6

Aleutian Showdown: Two Ships in a Death Grip

It's July 29, 1942. Fitted with big deck guns for protection against enemy ships, the Japanese cargo ship KANO MARU arrives at Holtz Bay, Attu Island, Alaska, a remote Aleutian island that the Japanese have occupied in order to divert US naval resources away from Midway and thereby divide the US Navy. The occupation marks the first time in history that US soil has been occupied by a hostile foreign power. The KANO MARO's mission is to bring supplies to Japanese troops on both Attu and Kiska Island, both of which are occupied by troops who have dug extensive tunnels and trenches to defend their positions. The captain and crew of the KANO MARO have no idea of ordeal they are about to face.

The KANO MARU takes on cargo and leaves for Kiska Island, escorted by sub chaser CH-26. Later that day, contact with the sub chaser is lost in a thick fog of the Bering Sea.

July 30, 1942. The KANO MARU approaches Kiska Island, but heavy fog prevents her from entering Kiska Harbor. She drifts far off shore.

SHIPWRECKS

As the fog begins to thin out, KANO MARU heads toward Kiska Harbor at 15 knots.

Meanwhile, the American submarine USS GRUNION is on her first war patrol. When she reports antisubmarine activity, she is ordered back to Dutch Harbor.

USS GRUNION surprises the KANO MARU, launching a torpedo that hits the machinery room of the Japanese cargo ship. Two Japanese sailors are killed. The starboard machinery room floods, and the diesel engine shuts down.

The KANO MARU remains afloat although she now lacks engine power. When the Japanese crew spots a periscope, they open fire with their big 40-calibre 3-inch guns. No hits are scored.

On the USS GRUNION, LtCdr Abele fires another torpedo, but Mark-14 torpedoes are unreliable. This one passes beneath the KANO MARU. The GRUNION fires two more, scoring two hits, but both torpedoes fail to explode. It is a devastating moment for Abele and his crew.

Faced with the prospect of failure, Abele takes bold and courageous action. He orders the GRUNION to surface, where the crew attempts to sink the disabled KANO MARU with gunfire.

The KANO MARU also has guns, however. Her crew opens fire on the GRUNION. One shot hits the GRUNION's conning tower. The GRUNION dives. Abele's crew loses depth control. The GRUNION plunges into the deep.

She exceeds crush depth and implodes in the freezing Bering Sea waters. Sudden death claims every crew member.

Later, sub-chaser CH-26 ISHIZAKI and cable-layer ship UKISHIMA arrive on scene. The crewmen spot debris from the doomed USS GRUNION floating on the surface. A crew from ISHIZAKI boards the KANO MARU to assist with repairs.

A Japanese transport ship attempts to tow the KANO MARU back to the *relative* safety of Kiska Harbor, but the towing cable breaks. The KANO MARU drifts all night in the lonely and hostile Bering Sea.

The next day KANO MARU is towed to Kiska Harbor where her cargo is offloaded.

The US aerial bombardment of Kiska Island continues. On the day of her arrival, two bombs explode near the wounded ship. She sustains hull damage from a near miss on her port side.

An Aleutian storm drives the KANO MARU against the coast. More than a mile SW of Kiska Harbor, she runs aground at the base of an eighty foot cliff. She is deemed beyond repair and abandoned.

The USS GRUNION is never heard from again. Back at the Dutch Harbor Naval Operating Base, her fate is unknown. She has simply disappeared in the vast gray waters around the Aleutian Islands, a chain that stretches a thousand miles from the Alaskan peninsula toward Russia's Kamchatka.

After more than six decades at the bottom of the Bering Sea, the USS GRUNION is found in 2006. She is found north of Kiska Island at a depth of more than 2000 feet. She is found by the fishing vessel AQUILA, which is towing a sidescan sonar, which is being used in the search for the GRUNION. The search is led by the two sons of the GRUNION's Commander Abele.

SHIPWRECKS

The shipwreck of the KANO MARU remains on Kiska Island, Alaska.

Today, there are many shipwrecks on Kiska Island.

Roger Weston's action-adventure novel, *The Golden Catch* is set on Kiska Island, which is one of the most remote islands in the world. The island also has one of the most hostile environments due to the Aleutian storms.

CHAPTER 7

World War II's Worst Shipwreck

A blacked-out German ship plowed through the frigid Baltic Sea on a deathly-cold January night in 1945. She was ferrying her passengers to safety from the Russians. World War Two was ending. Germany had fallen, and the Russians were rampaging across Germany, hungry for revenge against every man, woman, and child they found. Millions of panicked Germans had fled for Baltic ports, hoping to catch an evacuation ship and save their lives. Many people were not fortunate to find a place on a ship.

The *Wilhelm Gustloff*, a former cruise ship then hospital ship was currently ferrying 9,000 through the cold night. The 9,000 were mostly women and children. Many of the women were aged between seventeen and twenty-five. They were happy to be onboard after hearing so many accounts of rape by Bolsheviks. These fanatics were raping German women. While it's true that they had legitimate grievances against Germany, the women and children did not deserve this kind of treatment. Many of them did not even support their insane leader.

The women on board the ship were fortunate to escape from the Bolsheviks, but the *Wilhelm Gustloff* had been out of service for some time. One thirteen-year old boy was excited to be on the ship, but he was disturbed to see that ten of the lifeboats were missing. The rest were buried in snow. All the ropes were frozen, and nobody was clearing them.

Life boats or not, the women were fortunate to be on this ship—any ship. The alternative was horrible.

But one woman named Annie Faust saw it differently. She had a premonition of disaster, and she was heard saying, "I won't go on that death ship. I don't want to go on the *Gustloff*."

Unfortunately, she had no place else to go. She was stuck on the ship of her nightmarish vision.

One boy named Gunther was excited to be on the huge vessel, but he was disturbed when he saw that ten of the lifeboats were missing. The rest were buried in snow. All the ropes were frozen, and nobody was clearing them.

Although the thirteen-year-old boy Gunther was disturbed by the sight of the snow-covered lifeboats, he might have been even more concerned had he know that it was captain's orders that the lifeboats be kept inboard. They were not swung outward on their davits, which would have made them easier to deploy. Wartime rules said that they should be outboard. They were not.

When Gunther looked out over the waters passing by, he saw chunks of floating ice. He hoped they didn't need to use the lifeboats.

There were other problems that Gunther knew nothing about. For example, the *Gustloff* was a slow ocean liner, which made it more likely a prowling Russian sub could sink it. Plus, it was having engine problems, which slowed it further. The captain wasn't worried about floating ice. He was worried about floating mines, but that wasn't all. Captain Zahn ordered that the navigation lights be turned on to avoid a collision, perhaps with a minesweeper. The lights made the ship an easy target. In addition, he was not zigzagging the ship as was protocol to foil attacking submarines.

In addition to these safety issues, the passengers were not physically comfortable during this night cruise. The ship was literally packed with 9,000 people. It was hard to move around. Getting to the lavatories was an ordeal. They were clogged and smelled badly if you could get through. People were sick. An unpleasant smell filled the corridors. Of those who had life preservers, many took them off due to discomfort and body heat. The ship was surprisingly warm for a night when it was extremely cold outside.

Meanwhile a Russian submarine launched torpedoes. Three of them struck the *Gustloff*. Glasses and plates crashed to the floor in the officer's cabin. Water rushed through the engine room. The ship heeled over to starboard, then lurched over to port.

The radio officer sent out an SOS signal. He said, "*Wilhelm Gustloff* sinking. Position –55 degrees 07 North; 17 degrees 42 East. Please help." Unfortunately, it was a weak radio, and it didn't get through to naval headquarters. It was also the wrong frequency. These mistakes would be paid for in human lives.

Young Gunther was lying in his bunk reading when the explosions rocked the boat. He immediately went in search of his parents. When he found them, they proceeded up on deck in the midst of a panicked crowd. Women and children were crying. In parts of the ship, the cries were about to turn to screams.

From the wheelhouse, Captain Weller ordered the watertight bulkheads near the blasted hull be sealed off. That would slow the spread of water, but it also condemned some passengers to drowning. They could not escape.

The passageways were death zones where people who fell got trampled, including children. The lucky ones made it up on deck.

Or were they lucky?

Sigrid Bergfeld gave up the last seat in a lifeboat to a woman with a baby. This kind act was rewarded with a scene of horror. As the boat was lowered into the sea, waves promptly capsized it. The people were dumped into the icy sea, which was a death sentence. The average life expectancy in these freezing waters was just a few minutes—if you could swim.

After struggling through a crowd of desperate women and scared, clinging children, Sigrid approached another lifeboat in time to watch as it was lowered toward the water. Suddenly, the ropes fowled; the boat tilted and spilled its passengers into the sea. Bodies splashed. Screams and shrieks of horror filled the air.

Other passengers couldn't even launch their boats. The blocks and tackles were frozen solid with ice. Crewmen worked hard to remedy this because they had the rest of their lives to solve the problem. They learned that they had reservoirs of creativity and tenacity that they hadn't previously known about. One man was so motivated and determined that he used his bare fists as ice breakers.

As boats were lowered, people on the lower decks reached out and begged for help, but the people in the lowering boats could do nothing. Some desperate people leapt into the sea. They had few choices. One of these jumpers was the ship's barber. Business had been very good for him lately. As a result, he was carrying a bag of heavy coins strapped to his back. There was no way he was leaving his money behind. When he hit the sea, that extra weight quickly dragged him beneath the waves and straight to the bottom.

Meanwhile on the ship, a calm voice droned over the loudspeakers: "The boat will not sink. Rescue ships are on the way." For those who saw death closing in, they wanted to believe.

As the calm speaker gave these assurances, the ship shuttered and healed over. Dozens of people were dumped into the freezing Baltic Sea. The girl who had the premonition realized that she had been right. The nightmare was real. She should have heeded its warning.

In the wheelhouse, despite a slanting deck, Commander Zahn brought out a tray with glasses. "A final cognac, gentlemen?" The officers downed their last cognac. Then glasses shattered.

The ship heeled over more. Waves were hitting the funnel now. For no reason, the ship's sirens began to sound. It was a haunting thing to hear for those in the water. Then the ship slipped beneath the surface, carrying with it thousands of souls. In the place where the passengers had disappeared beneath the waves, swimmers saw air bubbles burst through the surface. The water looked as if it was boiling when it fact it was cold enough to make ice. As she plunged, the boiler exploded and the emergency lights came on. All of those with their heads above water could see the doomed, well-lit ship, even as it fell into the deep.

This was one of the last things that many of them ever saw in this life. The unbearable cold soon claimed them. Their physical struggles ceased. The water took them. For others, on the surface, the painful struggle for life continued. When people tried to climb into overloaded boats, the boats began to sink. The passengers had no choice but to beat the person until they let go. People were clubbed when they tried to save themselves. Some were even shot.

Dead bodies floated past the lifeboats. Many bodies.

Two boats, the *T36* and the *Hipper,* arrived to rescue survivors. They did what they could. One woman who was rescued tried to jump back in the water. She was distraut over having lost all her children. Numerous mothers who had lost their children were saved only to die of grief.

Petty officer Werner Fisch was serving on naval dispatch boat *VP1703* when they spotted a raft. He jumped in and found that, yes, the raft was full of people, but they were frozen people—dead and frozen. Werner did find one survivor, however. A baby was tucked under one of the ice-hard bodies. They took the baby on board, warmed him, and revived him. The baby was now an orphan, and Werner later adopted him.

Around 9,000 people died in the sinking of the *Wilhelm Gustloff.* That's five times more fatalities than the *Titanic*. It is considered to the worst maritime disaster in history.

Note: The *Wilhelm Gustloff* shipwreck is featured in the novel *Fatal Return* by Roger Weston.

CHAPTER 8

The Forgotten Rescue

In March of 1907, a ferocious storm raked the gloomy waters off the Cornish coast. Thick fog buried the Lizard peninsula. This treacherous outcrop was the home of many small fishing communities. On this night in the Ides of March, a fisherman's wife spotted an ominous red glow in the fog. Word spread quickly in the small community. Bearded fishermen leapt into action. It was clear that this red glow was no weather phenomenon. It was the distress flare of a ship. The news could not have been grimmer given that the conditions were brutal, and the chances seemed high that some if not all of the mysterious ship's passengers would die if they were not soon rescued.

The fishermen of the Lizard Peninsula knew the sea like nobody else alive, but on this night the sea raged out of control. The men knew the ferocious power of storms as surely as they knew the frailty of men in peril. They knew the code of the sea demanded their action. Four crews of men took to the oars of four rescue boats and set out into the wind-raked waters in fog so dense they could see nothing at all. In these eerie conditions, they rode the wild horse of the sea's towering waves. Huge waves thrust them high in the fog and they could see nothing but the distant red glow. They rose and fell, rose and fell. The men fought with all their might against a powerful south-westerly gale. The rowers pulled with all their might and even then could barely make progress against the adversity of the storm and sea. They were determined, however. Their will was fixed to match that of the sea. So thick was the fog soup that they couldn't see the stricken ship until the rescue boat bumped into her wave-swept hull.

As the waves heaved past the ship, which was run aground on a reef, the rescue boats were lifted high up toward her rails where 524 terrified passengers prayed for their lives. These included 85 children. When the rescue boats rose on the crests, men and women dropped their children overboard into the lifeboats. Two of the ship's own lifeboats had already been launched and were headed for certain doom because they did not know how to pass through the reef. The timely arrival of the local fisherman played a crucial role in their salvation. Another minute and they'd have been lost in the fog, lost to the hungry sea whose appetite is never satisfied.

All night long the men of the local fishing villages risked their lives, running out to the ship and rescuing loads of passengers. Sixty local fishermen took turns at the oars. Every passenger was ferried safely to shore where the wives of the fishermen had lit bonfires to guide their men home and keep the survivors warm.

These selfless local heroes worked all through the night, fighting a Herculean battle against the weather, making run after run out to the ship. These brave men, guided by a red glow on the waters and an orange glow of fires ashore, these men who knew the ways of survival at sea—they saved everyone on board, brought them all to safety. These men of the Lizard Peninsula were true heroes, and it is only fitting that their heroic deed should be remembered.

The ship was the *Suevic*, a 550-foot leviathan, her bow run aground on a reef. She survived the night as it turned out, but after the storm settled, neither her crew nor salvagers could get her to budge. There was no way to refloat her.

Almost no way.

There is always a way, and salvagers put forth a highly-risky plan to her owners, the famous White Star Line. What the salvagers proposed was to carefully place numerous explosive charges of dynamite up and down the sides of her bows. They would detonate all the explosives and sever the grounded bow from the rest of the ship. The rear 400 feet were not damaged, so the majority of the ship would be floated back to harbor, her compartments sealed off so that sea water would not flood her holds.

The explosives were detonated as planned, weakening the steal that connected the bow with the rest of the ship. That weakness gave way as the ship lifted and lowered on the watery swells. The ship—minus her bow, was sailed back to Southhampton under her own power. She was towed by salvage ships, but their role was mostly to guide the ship, since her engines and propellers were in good shape and provided the power for the voyage.

Back in port, her owners had a new bow built and attached to the ship, which was then in fine condition to continue her career on the high seas. In fact, she went on to sail for more than three decades, but was finally sunk by her crew to avoid her falling into the hands of the Nazis.

One final fact regarding this amazing tale should be mentioned. Two years after the wreck of the *Suevic*, her owners, the White Star Line, began work on another ship which was destined for a much more tragic shipwreck. That ship was the *SS Titanic*.

CHAPTER 9

The Shipwreck and the Lighthouse
July of 1865

Riding low in the water, carrying 244 passengers and crew, the side-wheeler, the *S.S. Brother Jonathan,* was en-route from San Francisco to Portland, Oregon. Her passengers, including dignitaries, settlers, freed slaves, prospectors, and a group of women living very hard lives—enjoyed first-class accommodations. Her cargo included gold. The 221-foot steamer got as far north as the Rogue River, but out at sea, the storm was fierce. Wind blew with wild abandon, carrying sheets of rain in a massive downpour. Waves tossed the ship and crashed over her decks. She sank down into deep, watery valleys, and when she rose on big swells, she took the full force of the wind.

Fear gripped the hearts of many passengers and crewmen. As the *S.S. Brother Jonathan* pressed on, nature flung her unbridled wrath at the ship. Wind howled through the rigging. The hull creaked and moaned, and passengers feared she would break up. Anything not bolted down was thrown about. In the galley, plates flew out of storm shelves and shattered on the floor. Pots and pans crashed. The noise was tremendous. Sea sickness spread like the black plague. Passengers were getting sick all over the place, and the smell belowdecks was not pleasant. Children cried.

Finally, the captain made a dramatic, fateful decision. He would turn the boat around and head back to Crescent City, California to find shelter. The *S.S. Brother Jonathan* had Crescent City within her grasp when a particularly large swell lifted her on high. She then swooped down into the ensuing trough where an underwater granite spire punctured her hull, opening up a geyser inside the paddle wheeler. Water began to fill the ship.

The crew worked vigorously to deploy the lifeboats, but it in those wild seas, it was perilous work. They successfully launched the first boat. However, she'd barely cleared the *S.S. Brother Jonathan* when a breaker capsized her, dooming 40 passengers who just moments before had thought themselves saved from the sinking ship.

Shocked and horrified, the crew had no time to mourn. There were more passengers to save and precious little time to save them. Crewmen struggled to keep their balance on the *S.S. Brother Jonathan*'s tilting, shifting decks. Wind threatened to knock them down or blow them overboard. Salty spray blew in their faces as they worked.

As they lowered the second lifeboat, a moment of surreal horror registered in their brains as they watched a wave crush the lifeboat against the hull of the *S.S. Brother Jonathan*. Helpless to save another boatload of their fellow voyagers, the remaining crew and passengers watched them perish right before their eyes. The violent ocean devoured them. Onboard the *S.S. Brother Jonathan*, people who hadn't prayed in years did so now with passion and urgency. One passenger wrote out his will. Others took stock of their lives. Their ordeal dragged out for 45 minutes, after which the *S.S. Brother Jonathan* sank like a rock.

One boat was successfully launched, and it carried nineteen people to shore. As those passengers reached land, they were gripped with conflicting emotions. There was thanksgiving and a level of appreciation for life that they had never known before. Men and women crawled on the sand and wept. A creeping sense of guilt touched some of them because they had lived while so many others had not. Out of 244 good people, those nineteen were the only survivors.

After the storm, bodies washed up the shores of Northern California and Southern Oregon. One of the bodies was that of James Nisbet, the man who'd written out his will on the sinking ship. His will was recovered from his pocket and later the terms were carried out. Many bodies washed ashore. These bodies brought news to Oregonians, sad news, news of life and death, of tragedy and warning. Such tragic news from the *S.S. Brother Jonathan* was not expected. She was known for bringing good news. Only six years previously, in 1859, the *S.S. Brother Jonathan* had brought Oregonians news that she had been admitted to the union as 33rd state. Often she brought gold from the goldfields of California. In fact, she was carrying a payload on this trip. Some say she was overloaded with cargo, which is why she rode low in the water. Her cargo included mill machinery, mining equipment, horses, and even two camels. Part of that cargo was a treasure chest of gold. Her cargo also included rare San Francisco gold coins that had been minted the year of the shipwreck, 1865.

Such statehood, however, would not matter in the futures of the lost passengers of the *S.S. Brother Jonathan*. Such gold counted as nothing to them now. Their bodies washed up on the beaches, carried there by life preservers that could not save them from hypothermia in the freezing waters.

In 1865, this ranked as the deadliest shipwreck so far on the Pacific Coast.

SHIPWRECKS

For decades, nobody knew exactly where the ship had gone down. However, in the 1930s, a fisherman hauled up a grimy load. It was an old metal lifeboat from the *S.S. Brother Jonathan*. Inspecting his catch, the curious fisherman found a rotten leather valise that was jammed under one of the seats. When he opened the valise, he was stunned. It contained twenty-two pounds of gold. In his career as a fisherman, this was one of his most exciting catches. It was a gift from the long-lost shipwreck, the *S.S. Brother Jonathan*. It's hard to explain how leather could last 70 years underwater. Perhaps it's one of the mysteries of the sea. Perhaps the fisherman got his story wrong. Probably, we will never know. At the time, private ownership of gold was illegal, and the fisherman secreted away his catch, sealing his lips, and keeping his mouth shut about his rare find. Later on, his memory failed him. He could not even recall the exact location where he'd netted the lifeboat.

In 1993, a treasure hunting expedition carried out by Deep Sea Research found the wreckage at a depth of 250 feet with the help of a mini sub. She was found fully two miles from the best estimates of the shipwreck's location. That she had moved so far underwater was attributed to the air pockets within the ship and the powerful currents. In 1996, DSR salvaged 1,206 gold coins. These were $20 Double Eagle gold coins in near-mint condition. Some of these coins can be purchased even today.

Government bureaucrats threatened legal action against DSR unless they were paid off. DSR settled by turning over 200 coins to the State of California. DSR was left to pay for the search that had led to the discovery. The coins were auctioned off and brought in $5,250 each.

Today in Crescent City, California, one can visit the Brother Jonathan Cemetery and Memorial; however, the memorial is not the only legacy of the *Brother Jonathan*. There is another, and on a clear day, it can be seen six miles off shore. It is the St. George Reef Lighthouse, which was constructed after the *Brother Jonathan* shipwreck. The beacon is situated on the Dragon Rocks of St. George Reef. Its purpose was to warn mariners of the rocks and thereby prevent another tragedy like that of the *S.S. Brother Jonathan*.

The St. George Lighthouse has stood tall and endured almost a century of powerful, frightful winter storms, yet her light continues to shine. During that time, four lighthouse keepers have been killed on the job. Service at St. George Lighthouse was considered to be the most dangerous assignment of the lighthouse service. The lighthouse is built on a low-lying, wave-thrashed rock, and even today, it is not safe for a boat to attempt a landing here. Operations were ceased in 1975; however, a group called the *St. George Reef Lighthouse Preservation Society* is dedicated to its maintenance and continuation. Thanks to their efforts, the light shines on.

    Built on a wave-washed rock, the base of the lighthouse consists of hundreds of granite blocks, which are able to endure the eternal pounding of the crashing surf. The tower rises 150 feet above the water and is topped off with a cast-iron lantern room, which today, thanks to the St. George Reef Lighthouse Preservation Society, is fully automated. Even today, sailors and fishermen are kept safe by the light.

CHAPTER 10

The Doomed Steamship *Lexington*

On the evening of January 13, 1840, the paddle wheels of the steamship Lexington thrashed the icy waters of Long Island sound. Originally commissioned by Cornelius Vanderbilt, the ship was carrying approximately 145 passengers and a cargo of baled cotton, which was stacked on deck. Running a route between New York and Stonington, Connecticut, she was one of the most luxurious steamers of her time.

Midway through the ship's latest voyage, the casing around the ship's smokestack caught fire, igniting nearly 147 bales of cotton that were stored nearby. Crewmen reacted by rushing below decks to try and stop her engine. This mission failed and gave the flames time to spread. Next, the crew made every effort to extinguish the flames. The neck muscles of crewmen bulged like ropes as they heaved buckets of water upon the flames. Unfortunately, the freezing wind fanned the blaze, and the crew fought a losing battle.

Realizing that the ship was lost, the crew reverted to evacuation protocol. Then a combination of deadly factors combined to create a disaster. With the engine still running, the first boat was sucked into the paddle wheel, smashing it to pieces and dooming all aboard, including the captain, who had fallen in by accident.

With the paddle wheeler still underway, panic and anxiety onboard only increased among the unfortunates who were seeing their joyful cruise turn into a nightmare. Passengers piled into the lifeboats, promptly overloading them. The crew then lowered the life boats too fast, and worse yet, the lowering ropes were improperly cut so that the boats hit the moving water at a tilt, turning them into the equivalent of big spoons dipped into the punch bowl. The life boats promptly filled with frothing ice water, and clutches of frigid death took hold. Immersed in the freezing drink, the poor souls fought off hypothermia as long as they could, but they lost the fight and sank into the cold depths of January.

Desperate passengers realized that death was closing on them too. They began heaving furniture and cotton bales into the water. These would have to do as makeshift rafts no matter how perilous the option.

At 8:00 p.m., *a passenger who was also a ship's captain by profession, a man called Captain Hillard, threw ten bales of cotton overboard and then jumped onto one of them. One of the ship's firemen also gained hold on the same bale. Together these two men floated in the open waters on their makeshift raft, on the greatest adventure of their lives. With a wind chill factor running below zero, they floated and slowly succumbed to hypothermia. The bales rose and fell in the pulsating waters of a dark night in the depths of winter. Stinging cold waves continually splashed them, keeping their body temperatures at dangerously low levels.* Around 4:00 a.m., Cox, overcome by hypothermia, slipped into the water and drowned. Hilliard, also weakened, nonetheless, held on tight. At 11:00 a.m., a sloop named *Merchant* swung up alongside and rescued Hilliard. The man they dragged out of the sea was insensible. He was clinging to life by a thread, but clinging fiercely.

At midnight, Stephen Manchester, the ship's pilot, and several other passengers were driven off the *Lexington* by the terrifying approach of intense heat and flames. Manchester and the others put to sea on a makeshift raft but the overloaded debris sunk beneath them. Driven by knifing cold and desperation that ran through his blood, Manchester, clawed at a bale of cotton and dragged himself out of the water like a wet dog. He and a passenger named Peter McKenna held on for dear life, but after a grueling three hours, McKenna gave up the ghost. Despite having death for company, death beckoning him to give up the fight, death taunting the weak with her torments, Manchester held on. He clung to life for hours beyond what mortal man could hope for. He was rescued by the sloop *Merchant* at noon.

Charles Smith, the ship's fireman, had every intention of outwitting the fire and saving his life. He and four other people clung to the Manchester's rudder where they had safe distance from the raging fires above them. Finally, as the ship began to sink into her watery grave, Smith and his fellow passengers climbed onto a piece of the paddlewheel, which was rising and falling in the choppy ice water. Death climbed onto the paddlewheel with them, and during the night she claimed souls one-at-a-time. Only Smith held out against her temptations. She offered an end of the suffering, but Smith had a purpose. Something drove him to endure all misery and share the night with hypothermia's oppressive company. The next day at 2:00 p.m., the sloop *Merchant* eased up by the paddlewheel and fished the half-dead fireman off his floating debris.

Another man who spit in Death's face was second mate David Crowley. On a bale of cotton, he drifted for 43 hours, pulling off the impossible, enduring beyond the accepted limits of human endurance, proving beyond all doubt that with grit and determination, man can accomplish far more than he realizes. Crowley also made a couple of key moves. He burrowed into his bale of hay and stuffed his clothes with cotton. After an amazing adventure, he drifted ashore, 50 miles east, at Baiting Hollow, Long Island. Despite all weakness, despite the fragility of life, he'd hung on until Providence smiled on him. The torments of dehydration had failed to finish him off. Hypothermia had not finished her work. David Crowley crawled up the beach. Then he managed to stand on shaking joints. Breathing in gasps, he staggered down the beach for over a mile, collapsing several times along the way. At home of Matthias and Mary Hutchinson, he knocked on the door and then fell against it, sinking to the deck, where he balled up and shook feverishly. The door was opened. The doctor was called.

It was reported that the celebrated poet Professor Henry Longfellow likely perished on the Lexington. Longfellow's works included "Paul Revere's Ride." While his name was listed on the manifest, he had backed out of the trip at the last minute to discuss a poem with his publisher, a poem about a shipwreck.

According to one report, the *Lexington* had been condemned several months before the fateful cruise, but the owners ignored this bad news and kept her in service. In fact, she'd had a fire on her last run, but *that one* had been put out. Interestingly, the captain of *that* cruise had called in sick, a move that probably saved his life. That captain was the brother of Cornelius Vanderbilt, who had originally commissioned the Lexington.

The Lexington had small fortune in silver below her decks, some of which was later recovered. While those salvagers had reason to smile, the families of 140 lost souls carried the memories of loss for many years.

CHAPTER 11

Mystery of the *Lusitania*

Allegedly, anonymous and mysterious telegrams were received by some passengers just before they boarded the fateful journey of a glamorous passenger liner that was to depart from New York on May 1st, 1915. The telegrams warned of impending disaster. They were signed *Morte*. Such was the beginning of the legendary final journey of the *Lusitania*, one of the most famous passenger liners ever. And in fact, she was about to play a stunning role in world history.

Officials denied the reports of the threatening telegrams. Evidently they were persuasive because 1,256 passengers decided to go ahead with the trans-Atlantic crossing to England—as well as hundreds of crew members. There were other reasons for caution, too. The German embassy in Washington, for example, warned travelers that it was wartime and ships like the *Lusitania* were legitimate targets. Keep in mind that due to the ongoing hostilities in Europe, crossings were limited. After all, the Germans were sinking ships with stealthy submarines called U-boats.

The passengers had plausible reasons to think that they would survive the dangerous trip. After all, the *Lusitania* was a fast ocean liner. Combine speed with the safety precaution of following a zigzag pattern and they might well have made it. Other ships certainly did. It was also said that no submarine could outrun the *Lusitania*, winner of the Blue Riband for being the fastest transatlantic liner. There were added factors that would inspire confidence. Passengers felt certain that the Germans would not hit a passenger ship—especially one with Americans onboard. If all of that wasn't enough, the ship's brochure advertized that she was "unsinkable". Many people have blind trust in authorities, and this claim must have given them comfort. The brochure also touted that the *Lusitania* and her sister ship were "the safest… in the world." This is a logical conclusion: an unsinkable ship would be safe indeed. These claims could be backed up, too. The ship was constructed with 175 watertight compartments, so that if one compartment was flooded, the others would stay dry, and the boat would be fine—assuming all the watertight doors were closed.

Furthermore, the famous multimillionaire Alfred G. Vanderbilt would be along for the crossing. Surely, if well-connected people were taking the trip, everything would be okay. Or would it? It is unlikely that the captain of the German U-boat knew or cared whether or not there were celebrities on board.

Amidst all the rumors and hype, the ship kept her schedule. She slipped her moorings on May 1st, and five days later entered dangerous waters. To his credit, the captain took several wise precautions in a display of competence and efficiency. The lifeboats were uncovered and swung out on their davits; the crew was told to have them ready for launch in case of trouble. He also dictated that the ship be blacked out, which was a wise move. He ordered extra lookouts on deck. Then on May 6th, the *Lusitania* received what must have been a chilling message over the wireless: *U-boat activity in the area.*

Anyone who has been at sea knows that this is not the kind of news that you want to hear. Nevertheless, the *Lusitania*'s captain was not especially concerned. This much can be inferred from his subsequent actions—or shall we say *lack* of actions. For example, the British Admiralty had issued critical instructions, which the captain either misunderstood or ignored. No doubt many passengers who signed on for the journey had taken comfort in the *Lusitania*'s capabilities. She was known for her speed, which meant they could outrun a submarine. There were other precautions a captain could take such as running a zigzag course. This made it difficult for a submarine to sink them. The passengers were right to think that these factors worked in their favor; however, the captain, as has been said, ignored such instructions. He also ignored the order to keep clear of headlands and steam in mid channel. He did the opposite. He ran a lackluster 18 knots, and he ran a straight course, hugging the coast a half mile offshore of the Coningbeg Lightship. He did all this in the very area where the submarines had been sighted. As a result, the *Lusitania* was an easy target.

At 1:20 p.m., a U-boat spotted the massive ocean liner and fired a torpedo, which struck the leviathan amidships. A second blast within the hull was even more powerful. This explosion in the boiler room was probably a detonation of the coal dust. However, the captain of the *Lusitania* had a secret. He was delivering more than just passengers to England; he was also delivering ammunition for the war against Germany. There were 5,000 cases of cartridges and 1,500 cases of shells. Furthermore, these were stored against the bulkhead leading into the No. 1 boiler room. Some have suggested that the ammunition caused the secondary explosion.

Either way, the damage was fatal. The ship listed to starboard. Within minutes, she tilted forward and buried her nose in the frigid water. Within 18 minutes, she made her descent to the bottom. Almost 1,200 doomed passengers and crew members made the deep fall with her; by the time the silt settled, they had surely passed on, and the ship had become their watery tombstone.

It may seem that this was a routine disaster where a ship was in the wrong place at the wrong time with the wrong captain. And that may be the case. However, there is a mystery associated with the *Lusitania*. Some writers have claimed that Winston Churchill, who was at the time *first lord* of the Admiralty, wanted this disaster. They have suggested that because there were over a hundred Americans aboard, their deaths at the hands of Germans would lure the Americans into the War. It is true that England was in dire straits and desperately needed military help from reluctant America. It is true that this disaster helped tilt the scales toward America entering the war, although not for a couple more years. While this is possible, at least for now, these claims are just conspiracy theories—at least until convincing evidence emerges, which so far has not yet happened after a hundred years.

On May 7, 1915, off the coast of Ireland, 1,198 people perished. These were mothers and fathers, sons and daughters. These people took a risk that didn't pay off. A hotel manager named Albert Bilicke took the cruise for his health because he was recovering from abdominal surgery. His recovery was cut short by the German torpedo. A 24-year old Canadian girl named Dorothy Braithwaite was on the *Lusitania* to visit her sisters in London, sisters who had been widowed on the same day. Dorothy never got a chance to console them. Emily Hadfield of Ontario, Canada, was traveling with her 8-month old baby. Emily perished in the shipwreck; however, her baby was plucked out of the water and survived. An opera singer named Millie Baker had been training her voice in France and Spain and was planning to make her stage debut with the Opera Comique, but she was deprived of her big chance. After her death on the *Lusitania*, her mother received a note in the mail, sent on May 1st, 1915, signed, "Love always, your Millie." Father Basil W. Maturin, stayed on the sinking ship and never attempted to board a lifeboat. Instead he gave absolution to all who requested it, and he handed a child onto the last lifeboat.

More than seven hundred survived the shipwreck. Many endured trauma and survived as a testament of the human spirit. They clung to floating debris and held on for their lives. One woman floated to shore in an armchair. Another woman gave birth in the water. She and her baby survived. A new bride was sucked into one of the funnels of the sinking ship, but was then spit out. She splashed down into the water near her husband's lifeboat.

As we are now beyond the 100-year anniversary of the tragic shipwreck, we honor and remember the passengers of the *Lusitania*.

CHAPTER 12

Shipwreck of Tears: The *SS Norge*

In 1903, a 37-year old Norwegian mother named Eline Sofie was on the most exciting trip of her life—a trans-Atlantic crossing on the passenger liner *SS Norge*. Along with her six children, she was sailing to America to join her husband and begin a new life in a country with more opportunity than anyplace else in the world. A fisherman named Jens Johansen Svartfjeld was also on board the ship. He was on his way to Minnesota along with his wife and five children.

On June 22, 1903, the *SS Norge* embarked from Copenhagen, Denmark under the experienced hand of Captain Gundel, who had sailed the ship since 1901. Onboard were 405 passengers from Denmark and a crew of 67. In Oslo, Norway, 232 passengers, including 70 children, came onboard for the journey across the Atlantic. All told, hundreds of people who were eager to start a new life in America were now passengers and closer by the hour to seeing their dreams come true.

There was no mystery as to why these people were going to the United States. It was a land of dreams, a place where people could start with nothing and achieve success. It didn't matter if they were born poor. Unlike Europe, anybody could improve their situation in America. It didn't matter what their status was. With hard work and ingenuity, anything was possible. To sail to America was like sailing on the clouds.

By the third day at sea, the excitement began to sink in. The sky was blue. The sea glittered. Passengers began to mingle and tell their hard-luck stories of entrenched poverty in Europe and share their dreams for the future. Some of them danced on deck.

That night, a number of travelers had a hard time sleeping due to their excitement, others because of the rough waters that had kicked up after dark. The boat was tossed around like a cork. Those who slept were jolted awake early in the morning, but not by the waves. A horrific crash shook the boat. The terrifying noise unleashed fear and dread in the hearts of the men, women, and children. Rudely awakened, they soon heard water sloshing around. Panic ensued as hundreds of half-dressed people ran for the upper decks. The decks were crowded, a mass of panic-stricken people who cried out in different languages when they realized they were on a sinking ship and the sea around them was actually their graveyard—and presently whispering their name.

A woman grabbed a crewman by the arm. "What's happening?" she begged.

"Nothing to worry about, *ma'am*. Calm down. We hit a rock. The captain knows what to do."

As people scrambled for life belts, the captain backed the ship off the rocks. No sooner had the ship regained headway when it was discovered that water was flooding the hold. This was called out in Scandinavian. A realization of imminent death stuck the hearts of the people. Fear swept over them and filled their souls with misery.

The sobs of old ladies filled the air. Screams added to the sense of panic. Women and children clung to each other. 240 Russians got down on their knees and prayed. Men wrung their hands. Little children cried.

The ship sunk lower into the sea as luggage and debris began floating on the decks.

Several quick-thinking men worked to free the life boats.

"Women and children first!" The captain's voice was barely heard over all the noise on deck, but some heard him. "Women and children first!"

Plenty of men ignored the captain if they heard him at all. They forced their way into the boats, leaving women and children behind on deck. One man who secured a spot was Fourth Mate Ankersen.

People continued to fight their way through the throng to get up front and secure a place. Many piled into overloaded boats. As a result, when the leaders tried to lower the boats into the water, the rusty equipment failed, dumping them all into the sea, rendering the boats worthless, dooming many souls.

Several of the life boats were properly deployed without exceeding their maximum loads. They now floated through a sea of drowning people—men, women, children, the suffering, and those unprepared to die, who certainly hadn't expected to die. People treaded water and begged for salvation. They realized that death had stolen upon them like a thief in the night. Their final minutes were ticking off as their light dimmed in the early morning. They called out for help, but nobody could help them. There weren't nearly enough life boats, and the ones in sight were filled to capacity. Oars dipped in the water as the fortunate ones on board rowed to distance themselves and save themselves. One overloaded lifeboat sank beneath the waves.

In other boats, people watched in horror as the *SS Norge* was also going down. The front end went under first. Then the stern sank, carrying hundreds of people into the frigid depths. The captain was one of those who went down with the ship. However, by some miracle, the sea spit him back up and he was picked up by one of the lifeboats.

People in the boats sobbed. They wept bitterly because of what they had just seen—and because members of their own families had been on the ship. Nobody could hear their cries, though, due to the fierce wind. The wind was especially fierce in the moments when the lifeboats crested on the huge, black ocean swells. Yesterday they had dreamed of America. Now they dreamed of land—any land. The only opportunity that mattered now was the opportunity to survive another day.

Survival—it had all come down to that. Just to survive and to live another day was a precious gift beyond imagination. Poverty? Hardship? These were minor concerns. Lack of opportunity? Nonsense. There was opportunity anyplace where a body could find land—opportunity to wrap oneself in a dry towel, to drink fresh water, to nibble on a slice of bread. That was opportunity of the most sublime type. Water, food, family, faith, and solid ground—nothing else mattered. All of the things they'd worried about now seemed totally irrelevant. They could not imagine that they'd worried over such petty cares as they had. It was all rubbish now—totally irrelevant.

On one of the lifeboats, Fourth Mate Ankersen took off his boots. "Use them to bail water," he said. He then jumped into the water. The others on the boat had just watched a man sacrifice himself so that they would have a better chance of survival.

On another boat, a brave young woman, Miss Petersen of Holte, Denmark, took the most dangerous spot as the craft rose and fell in the massive waves. She was constantly doused with freezing water. Thinly dressed, she ignored the cold. To her, suffering was irrelevant. Danger was nothing. She bailed frantically and all the while shouted words of encouragement to the others.

As the days passed, ships were spotted in the far distance. When sightings took place, an amazing thing happened on the boats. People that were previously demoralized and weak suddenly, as if by magic, regained their strength. Hope fueled them on the moment. Depression vanished into thin air to be replaced with excitement and adrenaline. But the people on the ships could not see the tiny life boats. The ships soon disappeared over the horizon. Now the same hungry, thirsty people became even more despondent than before.

The half-dressed survivors suffered through cold, wet nights. Fresh water was scarce, and thirst was a cruel tormentor. Some made the mistake of drinking salt water. Others cut themselves just to wet their miserable tongues and throats with their own blood. As the days passed, several of the children passed away. One who died was a Russian boy. His mother hid his body under her dress. She did this because she feared that the others would bury the child at sea. And this she would not allow. She steeled herself and held her boy close, protecting him from the pitiless ocean, determined to take him home.

The various boats drifted apart. Then, over the next week, five of them were rescued by different ships on different days over the next week. One was picked up after 24 hours. Others drifted for 5, 6, and 7 days. Three fully-loaded life boats were never seen again. They drifted into eternity.

What became of the 37-year old Norwegian mother named Eline Sofie, who along with her six children was traveling to America to join her husband in Minnesota?

The husband who anxiously awaited his young family never saw them again. Instead of a joyous reunion, of taking his wife in his arms and laughing with his children, he received the crushing news that his entire family had perished with the *SS Norge*, off Rockall Reef, two miles off the coast of Scotland. They were gone. They were only memories now. The cold Minnesota winters would be even colder for this man.

What about the fisherman named Jens Johansen Svartfjeld who was on his way to Minnesota along with his wife and five children? Their dreams all ended at sea. The entire family died. The last tears of the children fell into the salty sea.

Many families either lost several members or were wiped out completely. As of 1903, the *SS Norge* was the worst civilian maritime disaster in the history of the Atlantic Ocean. This was eight years before the wreck of the *RMS Titanic*.

Note: The investigation following the accident revealed several factors that led to the *SS Norge* disaster. They include the following:

a. The effect of the currents on their course was ignored. This proved to be a fatal oversight.
b. The full moon was also overlooked. The captain had turned southwards, but not far enough given the full moon and its effect on the tides. In reality, the ship was north of where the captain thought.
c. The captain chose to sail south of Rockall, a route mainly used by ships sailing east, so the *SS Norge* was at greater risk of collision. A safer route would have been better.
d. The captain chose to sail almost straight into Rockall so he could show it to the passengers. I doubt if the captain would have done that a second time. It's better to be responsible than popular.
e. The ship's life belts were mostly rotted
f. The *SS Norge* did not have nearly enough lifeboats.
g. The crew sailed at night without comparing the ship's position to the stars. They were unsure of their position.
h. The crew of the *SS Norge* had not drilled in emergency procedures. Therefore, when called upon, they were not ready.

Needless to say, the company shared some responsibility for the accident; however, the courts did not hold them accountable.

Books by Roger Weston

The Sands Series

GHOST SHIP: A Jake Sands Thriller **(Book 1)**

RELIC: A Jake Sands Thriller **(Book 2)**

THE TARGET: A Jake Sands Thriller **(Book 3)**

The Brandt Series

VENGEANCE: A Chuck Brandt Thriller (The Brandt Series Book 0)
The Recruiter: A Chuck Brandt Thriller (The Brandt Series Book 1)
The Handler: A Chuck Brandt Thriller (The Brandt Series Book 2)
Rogue Op: A Chuck Brandt Thriller (The Brandt Series Book 3)
Rogue Op II: A Chuck Brandt Thriller (The Brandt Series Book 4)
American Op: A Chuck Brandt Thriller (The Brandt Series Book 5)
Global Tilt: A Chuck Brandt Thriller (The Brandt Series Book 6)
Vulcan Eye: A Chuck Brandt Thriller (The Brandt Series Book 7)
Shadow Lawyer: A Chuck Brandt Thriller (The Brandt Series Book 8)
Shadow Court: A Chuck Brandt Thriller (The Brandt Series Book 9)

NonFiction by Roger Weston

SHIPWRECK: True Stories of Disaster at Sea

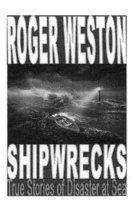

More Action-Filled Adventures by Roger Weston:

The Golden Catch: A Frank Murdock Action-Adventure

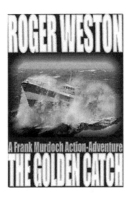

The Assassin's Wife: A Meg Coles Thriller

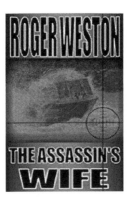

Made in the USA
Monee, IL
01 August 2021